A Gaijin's Guide

to the Japanese

Train System

A Gaijin's Guide to the Japanese Train System

Brian Breeding

As you move outside of your comfort zone, what was once the unknown and frightening becomes your new normal.

-Robin S. Sharma

A Gaijin's Guide to the Japanese Train System

Contents

1. Introduction..5

2. Getting Around...8

- Wi-Fi...............................9

- Applications......................12

- Maps................................14

3. Etiquette..17

- Line Up.............................18

- Lower Your Voice............19

- Silence Your Phone...........21

- Priority Seating..................22

- Food and Drinks......................23

4. Ticket, Smart Card or Commuter Card.....26

- Ticket..27

- Smart Card...............................30

- Commuter Pass.........................34

5. Train Punctuality...................................37

- Timetables...............................39

- Train Melodies........................41

6. Train Categories...43

- Local Train (Black)................45

- Raid (Red).............................46

- Express (Blue).......................47

A Gaijin's Guide to the Japanese Train System

- Limited Express (Green)........48

- Shinkansen (Bullet Train)......49

7. Additional Tips..53

8. Afterword..58

To my family and friends for making this research fun and exciting.

And to all of you who got lost with me over the years.

1

....

Introduction

It had always been a dream of mine to visit Japan. After having first stepped foot on island several years ago, I can still remember that overwhelming feeling of fear and confusion mixed with a sense of pure excitement. Living in Japan was going to be a challenge; I could not read, write or understand the language, other than the few phrases I had learned. Though the cards were stacked against me, I was determined to make my way through this beautiful country.

The train system is Japan's number one method of transportation and is known for its being highly efficient and extremely punctual. It is easy to be taken aback by everything going on around you, but having a solid understanding of the basics will set your mind at ease when you are standing in the station surrounded by the organized chaos.

In this book, you will find information and tips gathered not only from my personal experiences, but also from the experiences of tourists, expats, and railway veterans. It is my hope that after reading this you will be confident in your adventures through Japan and may be able to help someone along the way. Now, let's begin a gaijin's guide to the Japanese train system!

2

....

Getting Around

Before we make our way to the station there is one question I need to ask; how are you going to find your way? I ask this question since there are a few different methods to assist you in getting from start to finish. You could use a portable Wi-Fi device to use a directional application or you can be old-school and use a paper map of the train lines; choose whatever method works for you.

In this chapter we are going to be going over where to get a portable Wi-Fi device, the various applications you can use to get around and a breakdown of the train line maps. After reading this section you should be prepared to step off the plane or out of your hotel with a set path to reach your destination.

<u>Wi-Fi</u>

Finding free Wi-Fi in Japan is like finding a four-leaf clover, few and very far between. That being said, if you were planning on using

Wi-Fi to get around let me help. There are a few companies that offer portable Wi-Fi device rentals with varying data usage, maximum speeds and coverage.

For some, you may only need a SIM card to allow your device to work; depending if you already have a Docomo or SoftBank device. For those of whom do not, the portable Wi-Fi devices are our best choice. Depending on the company you choose, they can be ordered online and delivered to the airport or hotel of your choosing for pick-up.

Most companies allow their devices to be rented from one to thirty days with costs of ¥3,400 - ¥12,500, which roughly equates to $34 - $120 depending on the current exchange rate.

At those prices, being able to find your way, call home or upload all of your amazing vacation pictures seems like the way to go. Once you are done with your trip, returning your device can be as easy as using an envelope the company provided to mail it back to them.

If you are interested in renting a portable Wi-Fi device for your trip, here are a few companies that offer their services:

- Japan Wireless
- Sakura Mobile
- Fox Wi-Fi
- Pupuru Wi-Fi

Applications

Now that you have the internet back in your hands, you can figure out which application you are going to use to help find your way. I have tried many applications, but what works best for me may not work well for you. Instead of just telling you which application I use, I will be listing a few for you to try out and see which one you are more comfortable with. All of the applications listed below are available for both Android and Apple devices.

A Gaijin's Guide to the Japanese Train System

- **Google Maps:** Makes navigating your world faster and easier. Find the best places in town and the information you need to get there.

- **Hyperdia:** Offers detailed timetables, platform information, trip duration and exact distance, which will help you greatly in organizing your trips in Japan. The website and app are easy to use and understand, which will make all complicated travel plans a piece of cake.

- **NAVITIME:** A transfer information app that allows you to easily search for necessary information such as timetables and route information anywhere in Japan, easy to understand route maps, and the locations of boarding areas to transfer smoothly.

Maps

The map you see above may look confusing, but I assure you it will be quite easy to decipher after you have read this section. At a quick glance you see a bunch of colors, lines, shapes and words; all of those together equals a railway line. The map you see above is of the Yamanote Line, which is singlehandedly the easiest way to get around Tokyo as it stops at a vast majority of the major stations.

Let's break down this map, first we will cover the colored lines. There are three colored lines; green, red and yellow. Those represent the different rail lines with green representing the Yamanote Line, the red representing the Chuo Line and the yellow representing the Sobu Line.

The circles represent the various train stations along that rail line with a few lines intersecting at the same train station allowing for you to transfer to another rail line.

Lastly are the words themselves; as you can see some stations are bold while others are not. The bolded stations represent major stations along that rail line which are usual popular areas or major transfer stations.

Having an understanding of how the Japanese rail maps work have saved me countless times when I have been out with a dead phone or Wi-Fi device. If you ever find yourself lost and unable to decipher the maps, do not hesitate to ask an attendant for help. Simply telling them the station you want to go is usually enough to get some assistance.

A Gaijin's Guide to the Japanese Train System

3

....

Etiquette

Before we make our way to the station there is one question I need to ask; how are you going to find your way? I ask this question since there are a few different methods to assist you in getting from start to finish. You could use a portable Wi-Fi device to use a directional application or you can be old-school and use a paper map of the train lines; choose whatever method works for you.

<u>Line Up</u>

Once you have entered the platform, you are going to need to line up at the car of your choice. I will say that if you are looking to get a seat, the first and last car are your best choice as the middle tends to get quite crowded.

Note: The number of passengers on some trains in Japan can get to the point of being shoulder to shoulder.

Looking down you may find a number or kanji on the edge of the platform, those designate where the car doors will open. If a line has not formed, stand behind the number or kanji and wait patiently. Once a train has arrived, stand either to the left or right and allow the passengers to exit first before attempting to get on. If a line has formed, please stand at the end or near an area not blocking pedestrian traffic.

In some train stations there are colored boxes on the ground that represent the waiting area for the different types of trains; local, express, limited express, etc. Take a look at the electronic display showing the upcoming trains and it will tell you which box to stand in.

Lower You Voice

During your time in Japan, you are going to notice how respectful the Japanese people are and how much you are going to miss it when you leave. You can look around and see how tidy and clean everything is, to include how quiet it is. I have often found myself at the Shibuya Crossing and realize that I hardly hear any type of noise pollution. Everyone is keeping to themselves, only taking up as much space as needed and in a constant motion to get to their destination. Let's take this to the train.

When you get on the train you should move to your seat, if you can get one, and take up only enough space as needed. That means no man-spreading or placing your purse or bag next to you. If you have a bag, you can place it between your feet, on your lap or on the storage rack above you. Now let's talk about how we are used to speaking at a normal volume and how we should not do that on the train. Think of a time where you were out enjoying yourself when some obnoxious person was yelling about some nonsense; well in this case that would be you.

As you will see, the people on the train are doing one of a few things; staring at their phones, staring out of the window, talking closely to the person next to them or sleeping. Each individual person on the train is respecting the peace of everyone else. To sum it up; practice respect.

Silence Your Phone

Silencing your phone goes along with respecting the peace of everyone around you. It may seem like nothing, but it's a small gesture of kindness to the people who are just trying to decompress after a long day of work. Along with silencing your phone, attempt to avoid answering your phone during your ride. If it can be handled via text, try and do so. If you absolutely need to answer it, do so quietly.

<u>Priority Seating</u>

A Gaijin's Guide to the Japanese Train System

You may notice when you enter the train certain seating near the front and back of your car marked with yellow poles and hand-rings. That my friend would be priority seating.

Those seats are typically reserved for the elderly, disabled/injured, pregnant and people with small children. I say typically, because if the train is not too crowded and there is no one there fitting those descriptions then feel free to take a seat. Though I will stress if they do enter the train, offer them your seat.

<u>Food and Drinks</u>

Finding food and drinks on the go will not be difficult during your trip in Japan. There is usually a Family Mart, Lawsons, or 7/11 on every corner where you can pay your utility bills, grab the latest manga, and pick up some pretty awesome food.

While on the go, you may be tempted to take out your sandwich and Aquarius, but please refrain from doing so. Due to the sporadic movements of the train, it is possible that you may drop your food or drink causing a mess you may be unable to clean up.

As we have touched on before, Japan is known for being extremely clean. Simply waiting until you get to your next stop or destination before eating contributes to the continued reputation of having an immaculate public transportation system and also shows respect for the people around you.

4

....

Ticket, Smart Card or Commuter Pass

It's finally time to enter the station, but you are wondering how exactly you are going to do that. Worry not, because we are going to be going over a few ways to get you past the ticket gate and on to your train. In this section we are going to touch on the paper ticket, the IC cards and commuter passes, as well as, their advantages and disadvantages.

Ticket

As you may have guessed, a ticket is a paper, one use item. In order to obtain a ticket, you must visit an automated ticket machine located before the ticket gate and see how much it will cost to get to your destination. There will be a translated fare list to the left or right of the machine to help you. Once you have figured out how much your trip will cost, you must maneuver through their system to purchase your ticket. Fear not for they have translations for multiple languages and if all else fails, just ask an attendant for assistance.

Once you have your ticket, you are now able to insert it through the ticket gate and pick it up on the other side. Ensure you do not lose your ticket along the way. If you happen to lose your ticket, proceed to the exit and inform the attendant. They may ask where you boarded the train and how much the fare was, so do your best to remember. One of two things may happen from there, they may ask you to pay again or escort you to the exit.

So, let's say you bought a ticket thinking you needed to go one station, but actually needed to go to a station a bit farther. Well, you are going to have to pay a bit more on the backend. Once you reach your final destination, take your ticket to a ticket machine right before the exit and choose the 'Fare Adjustment' option.

A Gaijin's Guide to the Japanese Train System

Follow the directions on the display and you are all set!

Advantages

....

- Only spend how much it takes to get to your station.

- Able to be change fare later.

Disadvantages

....

- Time consuming due to using ticket machines.

- Tickets are easily lost.

Smart Card

A Smart Card is similar to the Oyster card in London. It is a self-loaded card that allows you to touch the automated ticket gate and keep moving with no fuss. I have come across two types of IC cards; the Pasmo and Suica cards.

You can purchase a Pasmo or Suica card at any participating ticket vending machine for ¥500, roughly $5, located outside of the station entrance. Once you get the display translated, you can then find the option to create your own card with or without your name typed on it. You will need to provide a little identifying information before your card is issued. If you are going to be in Japan for a short period of time, I would suggest getting a blank card. Once your card has been processed you can use the same machine to load it with Yen. As with a ticket, if you go too far and do not have enough loaded to leave the station you can walk over to the ticket machine before the exit and load it back up. It is always good practice to have extra yen on you.

Now let's say you have entered the station but forgot something and need to leave. In order to exit the station, you cannot leave the way you came in. First you must walk over to the attendant manning the gate and tell them you need to cancel your trip. They will ask you for your IC card and cancel your entrance enabling you to leave and enter the station again when ready.

When it's time for you to leave Japan, you can take that IC card to a gate attendant and tell them you would like to refund it. You can only get a refund on cards that your name has not been printed on. This way you will get whatever cash is on your card, as well as, what you spent in order to get the card back.

Note: You can also use your IC card to buy items out of certain vending machines.

Advantages

....

- Pre-loaded cards allows for faster commute.

- Cards are able to be loaded at any time.

- Can be refunded at the end of your trip.

- Can be personalized.

Disadvantages

....

- If lost, you are out of whatever money was on it.

- If personalized, cannot be refunded.

<u>Commuter Pass</u>

Commuter passes are similar to the regular IC cards but allow for unlimited use of the train lines along the route between your home station and your final destination. These passes are available to anyone and are mainly used for individuals who will be commuting on a set path each day; they are mainly used by students and people traveling to and from work.

In order to make a pass, you must first decide if you are going to be traveling on the JR line or Tokyo Metro, as the JR line creates Suica cards and the Tokyo Metro creates Pasmo cards. The only difference between the two are the companies that own them. They still function interchangeably between lines.

Once you have decided which card you want, you will need to visit their office located in the major stations. You will pay a flat fee for anywhere between one month to half a year. The commuter passes can still work similar to regular IC cards, though you will need to load them with yen to cover the exit fees.

Advantages

....

- Allows for unlimited transit along chosen route.

- Pre-loaded cards allows for faster commute.

- Cards are able to be loaded at any time.

- Will be personalized.

Disadvantages

....

- If lost, you are out of whatever money was on it.

- Cannot be refunded.

....

Now that you have an understanding of the ticket, IC card and the Commuter pass, you should be able to navigate entering and exiting the stations with ease. Remember the advantages and disadvantages for each and let your commutes begin!

5

....

Train Punctuality

The train system in Japan is known for being extremely punctual and without delay, minus a few unfortunate circumstances. As a testament to their unwavering ability to always arrive on time, you can find the train schedule on a sign within the station that may appear to have been there for years. That being said, if you are using Google Maps and the app tells you that your train will depart at 14:32; it's leaving precisely at 14:32. Thanks to this, many commuters have their trip down to a science. The peace of mind knowing that their trains schedule never changes allows them to focus on other tasks throughout their trip. In this section we will go over two topics to assist you in being on time.

A Gaijin's Guide to the Japanese Train System

Timetables

Whatever train station you enter, there will always be a timetable available to see when the next train will arrive and what type of train it is. It may be a digital display able to translate the words or it may be a flip display with minimal translations. Either way, with the help of your directional application you can play 'match the kanji' in order to see which train you are going to board. The accuracy of these timetables is the same throughout the station and on whatever directional application you are using.

Knowing the drop-dead time to get to your platform is paramount in situations as catching the last train from the station or boarding the Shinkansen, and at the very least know how much time you have left so you can buy a sandwich at the conbini.

Note: Conbini is the name for Japanese convenience stores.

A Gaijin's Guide to the Japanese Train System

Train Melodies

When standing on the platform there will be a moment where you ask yourself, "What are these sounds I'm hearing?". Barring anything unusual happening, you are probably referring to the train melodies. These various tones are notifications to the commuters to tell them that either a train is inbound or outbound, as well as, if the doors are opening or closing.

In Japan, the departing train melodies are arranged to invoke a feeling of relief in a passenger after sitting down and moving with the departing train. In contrast, the arriving train melodies are configured to cause alertness, in an effort to help travelers shake off sleepiness experienced by morning commuters.

6

....

Train Categories

At this point you are essentially a commuting professional, but we will go over just one more bit of information. There are a few different categories of trains you will need to know in order to make your trip as efficient as possible. Some trains stop at every station, some only stop at major stations and others stop at select local and major stations. To prevent you from wasting time, you will need to be able to board the right train.

A Gaijin's Guide to the Japanese Train System

Local (Black)

Local trains stop at every station along the route and can be identified two ways:

- Along with the destination the placard says 'Local'.

- The lettering is white written on a black background.

Use the local train if you have time to spare or to get to a station no other train will stop at.

Rapid (Red)

Rapid trains skip a few stations along the route and can be identified two ways:

- Along with the destination the placard says 'Rapid'.
- The lettering is white written on a red background.

The rapid train allows you to get to your station a little quicker.

A Gaijin's Guide to the Japanese Train System

Express (Blue)

Express trains stop at even fewer stations along the route and can be identified two ways:

- Along with the destination the placard says 'Express'.

- The lettering is white written on a blue background.

Some train companies may charge an express fee along with the basic fare.

Limited Express (Green)

Limited Express trains only stop at major stations along the route and can be identified two ways:

- Along with the destination the placard says 'Limited Exp.'.

- The lettering is white written on a green background.

Using the Limited Express train usually results in being charged a limited express fee along with the basic fare.

A Gaijin's Guide to the Japanese Train System

Shinkansen

The shinkansen is a high-speed train also known as the bullet train. Consisting of multiple networks across Japan's main islands, this train system is mainly used to travel long distances over a short amount of time. The shinkansen can reach a maximum speed of 320 km/h (200 mph). and is renowned for its punctuality, comfortable seats and its safe history. A common use is for traveling to and from Tokyo and Kyoto.

In order to travel via the shinkansen, you must purchase a ticket either at the ticket counter, machine or by using the preferred method, reserving tickets in advance using one of many websites.

Below are some websites you can use to purchase a ticket in advance:

- JR West
- JapanICan

- JR East
- Shinkansen Ticket

- Voyagin

A Gaijin's Guide to the Japanese Train System

There are three classes of seats offered which are usually found in separate cars; non-reserved, reserved and green seat.

- **Non-Reserved:** As the name suggests, these seats are purchased on a first come, first served basis.

- **Reserved:** These seats must be purchased in advance.

- **Green Seat:** These seats must be purchased in advance and cost more than Reserved seats as they are wider, providing the passenger with more comfort.

In order to make a seat reservation, you are going to need to provide the following information:

- Number of Travelers

- Date of Departure

- Station of Departure

- Station of Destination

- Class of Seat

Once you have your ticket, you can proceed through the ticket gate as normal.

7

....

Additional Tips

As much as I would like to cover every single facet of the train system, I decided I would only cover the basics. This guide will get you to your destination, but I figured I would leave us off with a few additional tips that should help.

Tip #1. The trains stop between midnight and 1AM.

- It is easy to lost track of time in this amazing country. Ensure you set an alarm to remind you to head to the station if you are going to stay out late. Taking a cab will be far more expensive than taking the train.

Tip #2. Bring a Condensable Stroller.

- As we have discussed, the trains can get packed. Having a condensable stroller will take up less space, but will also help you when it comes time to walk up the stairs to the restaurant or shop you want to visit. So, either bring a condensable stroller or a baby carrying system.

Tip #3. Find the Elevators.

- If you are a parent strolling your child around; ensure you find the elevators. Just as almost everywhere else, strollers are not allowed on the escalators. Just look for and follow the signs to your nearest one. If you cannot find it, just ask.

Tip #4. Learn a Few Phrases.

- It helps to know a few phrases to get you by. English can only get you so far, so embrace the culture and learn a bit. If all else fails, you can ask if they speak English.
- Do you speak English? "Eigo o hanasemasu ka?"

A Gaijin's Guide to the Japanese Train System

Tip #5. Avoid Rush Hour.

- Heading out in the morning or coming back in the evening? Try to avoid doing so between 0700 - 0930 and 1700 - 2000.

8

....

Afterword

It is my hope that this guide has answered your questions and has prepared you for transiting through the Japanese train system. Looking back, I remember walking through a bookstore looking for books to help me prepare for my trip. I grabbed phrase books, customs books and information covering all sorts of events that occur throughout the country, but now I wished I had grabbed a guide on the train system.

Doing so would have saved me from many embarrassing moments.

I wrote this book for people like me who want to prepare ahead of time and get a heads up prior to stepping into an uncomfortable situation. Even today there are times where I find myself having to stop and ask an attendant for assistance.

Do not be afraid to get out of your comfort zone. Plan your adventures, but be prepared when they completely fall apart. Walk around aimlessly and you may be surprised at what you may find.

Take care everyone and have fun!

一期一会

A Gaijin's Guide to the Japanese Train System

www.ingramcontent.com/pod-product-compliance
Lightning Source LLC
Chambersburg PA
CBHW062104290426
44110CB00022B/2710